Following You

Following You

Conversations with Jesus

Barbara Jurgensen

AUGSBURG ■ MINNEAPOLIS

FOLLOWING YOU
Conversations with Jesus

Copyright © 1990 Augsburg Fortress. All rights reserved. Except for brief quotations in critical articles or reviews, no part of this book may be reproduced in any manner without prior written permission from the publisher. Write to: Permissions, Augsburg Fortress, 426 S. Fifth St., Box 1209, Minneapolis MN 55440.

Scripture quotations unless otherwise noted are from the Holy Bible: New International Version. Copyright 1978 by the New York International Bible Society. Used by permission of Zondervan Bible Publishers.

Cover design: Eric Walljasper

Library of Congress Cataloging-in-Publication Data

Jurgensen, Barbara
    Following you : conversations with Jesus /Barbara Jurgensen.
      p.   cm.
    ISBN 0-8066-2502-3 (alk. paper)
    1. Jesus Christ—Devotional literature.   2. Imaginary
conversations.   I. Title.
BT306.5.J87   1990
242'.8—dc20   90-45251
                                                                                              CIP

The paper used in this publication meets the minimum requirements of American National Standard for Information Sciences—Permanence of Paper for Printed Library Materials, ANSI Z329.48-1984. ∞™

Manufactured in the U.S.A.   AF 9-2502

94   93   92   91   90   1   2   3   4   5   6   7   8   9   10

To
Dan, Dave, Jan, Marie,
Peter, and Phillip

With thanks to
Louise Kelling, Leslie Weichenthal,
Ralph Seager, Irene Getz, John Hanka

Contents

About This Book 9

The Welcome 11

What We Have 12

The Chosen 13

The One Who Comes 14

The Splitting 15

Following You 16

I Don't Feel Like Praying 17

Today 18

We Are the Needy 19

A Gift 20

We Give Thanks 21

Heal Us, Jesus 22

When Were Your Sorrows? 23

Assumptions 25

Entry 26

Morning Prayer 27

The Right Word 28

When the Storm Strikes 29

Calm Us Down 30

Restless 31

The Breaking of the Bread 32

It's Difficult 34

No Other 35

Outstretched 36

Believing 37

Dress for Success 38

The Donkey 39

The Troubled Family of Jesus 41

Well-being 43

Psalm 119:11 44

Places of Honor 45

The Call 46

Thank God for Friday 47

When We Look at the Cross 48

The Promise 49

Give Us 50

Perhaps 51

Hostility 52

I'm Afraid We've Thought . . . 53

The View from the Cross 54

A Person of Little Significance 55

My Biggest Fear 57

Letting Go 58	You Have Shown Us 70
Passersby 59	Pass It Along 71
The Two Jacobs 60	What Are You Doing Today? 72
We're Wondering 61	
Fishing 62	Because 73
What Would We Do? 63	Translation 74
From God 64	What Are We Doing? 75
Gifts 65	When 76
On That Day 66	At Harvest 77
Your Call 67	New Hope 78
Centering 68	We're Chosen 79
Necessities 69	It's Coming 80

About This Book

Lasers, computer databases,
and the glaring headlines of
grocery store checkout counter
tabloids provide topics for
these conversations with Jesus.
The One who spoke to people
in the language of their every-
day lives might like to talk
with us in a similar way today.

Join these conversations about
our anxieties and longings—
and about the hope given us by
the One who showed the extent
of his love for us one Friday.

The Welcome

Into our wildernesses
comes a voice
crying,
"Prepare the way
for the Lord!"

But how do we prepare?

Do we go into a frenzy
of trying to
straighten up things?

Or do we realize
there's too much of that to do
and give up?

Either way,
we'll never be ready.

But we say,
simply,
"Jesus,
come."

What We Have

Jesus, as we come
into your presence
we bring an offering
of all of our anxiety
and pain.

We bring our weaknesses
and struggles
and shortcomings.

They are not
what we would like to bring,
but they are what we have.

Maybe later we can
bring you better gifts.

For now,
we bring you these.

The Chosen

Jesus,
you have called us
your servants,
your chosen,
in whom your soul
delights.

Us, Jesus?

Us?

The One Who Comes

On the longest night
at the darkest hour
in the coldest part of the year . . .

To the lowliest barn
in the smallest town
in a land drawn tight in fear . . .

Came a tiny One
to a humble pair
who were far from all held dear . . .

On the longest night
at the darkest hour
in the coldest part of the year.

In the darkest hour
of the longest night
in the coldest part of our year . . .

When all hope has fled
and all light gone out
and our hearts are filled with fear . . .

Bringing hope and strength,
bringing purpose, life,
does the caring One appear . . .

In the darkest hour
of the longest night
in the coldest part of our year.

The Splitting

When you were baptized, Jesus,
as you began your ministry,
the heavens split open
and the Holy Spirit descended upon you
and God said, "You are my Son, whom I love;
with you I am well pleased."

When you were crucified
as you finished your ministry,
a great earthquake split the rocks.
The veil of the temple
was split from top to bottom
and you gave up your spirit
and the centurion said,
"Surely this man was the Son of God!"

And the great split
that separated us from you
and from those around us
was healed.

Following You

Jesus, life is very difficult,
   as you well know.

And we don't always do so well,
   as you well know.

But we have set our lives
   on following you.

And so we need you
   to walk beside us . . .

Or we will get off the path,
   as you well know.

I Don't Feel Like Praying

Jesus, I don't feel like praying today
because there's something I'm worried about.

> I understand.
> I agonized one night
> in the Garden of Gethsemane.

And I don't feel like praying
because I'm so angry about what someone has done.

> I was angry when I drove
> the moneychangers out of the temple.

And I don't feel like praying
because I'm so sad about something that's happening.

> I cried over the city of Jerusalem
> because they were unwilling to listen to
> the message I brought them from the Father.

So, Jesus, you can see why
I don't feel like praying today.

> I understand.
> But I would like to hear
> about the things that are making you
> worried and angry and sad.

Would you?
Could you possibly understand?

Today

Jesus,
today I walked past
someone who was hungry . . .

And ignored a person
carrying a heavy load . . .

And was too busy
for someone
in pain.

I think
I may have
walked past,
ignored,
and been too busy
for you.

We Are the Needy

We kneel before you,
Jesus, asking for your help.
You can make us clean.

A Gift

It is all God's grace,
not something that we do, that
makes us new in you.

We Give Thanks

We give thanks to you, Jesus,
not because *you* need it,
but because *we* do.

We give thanks to you, Jesus,
not because your heart craves it,
but because ours do.

We give thanks to you, Jesus,
not because you can't go on without it,
but because we can't.

Heal Us, Jesus

Jesus, we are blind
to the things
that are most important
in this world.

We are deaf
to the cries of those
who are troubled.

We are unable to speak
the words we should.

We are crippled
by centering our lives
in ourselves.

Heal us, Jesus.

When Were Your Sorrows?

O man of sorrows,
we know of your agony in Gethsemane
and during your trials
before Caiaphas and Pilate
and of your final agony
as you hung between heaven and earth.

But did you become acquainted with grief
earlier—
much earlier?

Perhaps sorrow came upon you after you were sent
to a young woman not yet married
and to her fiance,
who knew that you could not possibly be
his own child.

How were you,
a child born out of wedlock,
received in the little village of Nazareth?

Did mothers
warn their children
not to play with you?

Did they think Mary,
as the law decreed,
should have been stoned?

How did the men treat Joseph?
Did they say, "Sure, Joseph,
sure. It was the Holy Spirit"?

How did Joseph's parents feel
about this Mary
and about this little boy who was
not really their grandchild?

How did Mary's parents
treat her and her son?

Would the other women of the village
let Mary be a part of their get-togethers,
or was she surrounded by silence?

O man of sorrows
and acquainted with grief,
was there ever a time
when you knew no sorrows,
no grief?

Assumptions

We assume that rulers of nations
will live in palaces
and wear the finest of clothing.

But you, Jesus, chose rather
to begin your life on earth
in a stable,
and to wear the humble
windings of the poor.

We assume that rulers
will expect others,
especially their servants,
to cater to their every whim.

But you chose, rather,
to come among us
as yourself a servant
and care for our needs.

We assume that rulers
will expect to be treated royally,
with great pomp and consideration.

But you allowed us
to strike you
and spit upon you
and mock you
and finally nail you
to some hard planks.

Jesus, you move beyond
all our assumptions.

Entry

Jesus,
as we enter your house
we feel the tenderness
you have toward us.

We feel the forgiveness
you have brought us.

And we feel a pull
to follow one
who loves us so completely.

Morning Prayer

Jesus, please feed the hungry,
give shelter to the homeless,
and heal all who are
troubled and in pain.

Wait. Just a minute.
Are we asking you
to do the things
you've asked us to do?

The Right Word

It's hard to find the right word
to describe you, Jesus.

The word *humble*
doesn't say enough
about how simply
you live among us.

The word *gentle*
doesn't begin to speak
of how forgiving
and merciful you are.

And the word *caring*
can't begin to tell
of how you wrap your loving arms
around those of us
who are troubled.

When the Storm Strikes

Jesus, you set troubled hearts
at rest
when you spoke a word
that calmed the rage
of wind
and sea.

Speak a word
today
for us.

Calm Us Down

Calm us down, Jesus,
calm us way down.

So many voices
clamor for our attention
that we've become confused.

Calm us down
so we can hear your voice.

Restless

I'm not doing well
at casting all of my cares
upon you, Jesus.

The Breaking of the Bread

As they walked the road to Emmaus on that day,
Jesus walked with them—
and they asked him in to stay.
When he blessed the bread and he broke it,
    then they knew
that the news they'd heard
of his rising must be true.

> You were known to them in the breaking of the
>   bread,
> risen from the dead, risen as you'd said.
> You are known to us as the firstborn from the
>   dead
> in the breaking of the bread.

They had fished all night
and caught nothing, though they'd tried,
until Jesus came and said, "Fish the other side."
Then they cast their nets
and brought such a catch to shore;
he served bread and fish until they could eat no
    more.

In the upper room as they shared a simple meal,
Jesus came to them,
resurrected, yes, and real.
Then he took some fish and he ate it in their sight
and they knew the dark grave
could not hold the Lord of light.

> You were known to them in the breaking of the bread,
> risen from the dead, risen as you'd said.
> You are known to us as the firstborn from the dead
> in the breaking of the bread.

When we take the bread and the wine,
his gift of grace,
then we know he lives and prepares for us a place,
that he sends us forth—
spread the word from shore to shore
that in him we all have new hope forevermore!

As we share our bread with the hungry,
>> far and near,
may we share the One
who dispels our hate and fear.
May we share our bread and the Bread of Life
>> that he,
in a hungry world,
broken bread for all may be.

> You were known to them in the breaking of the bread,
> risen from the dead, risen as you'd said.
> You are known to us as the firstborn from the dead
> in the breaking of the bread.

It's Difficult

Jesus, we want to trust in you
and follow you,
but it gets difficult
when we have to do this
on faith alone.

We can't see you
or hear you
or touch you.

We can't use any of our five senses
to get to know you
as we could to know anyone
or anything else
in this world.

But, we know that we hear you
speaking to us in your Word.

And in your Word we see you
as you go about
preaching to the crowds,
teaching small groups of followers,
healing the sick and the troubled.

And we can taste
and smell
and touch
as we take the bread and the wine,
your body and blood given for us.

No Other

Jesus, no other faith
has anyone like you,
because no one
could have imagined
that a god,
or the child of a god,
would want to come to earth
and do what you did.

We think of gods as
self-important,
demanding to be honored.

We could not
have imagined
someone like you.

Outstretched

They stretched you up
high on a hill,
out beyond the edge of the town—
thinking they were done with you.

But they only made it easier,
from that high place,
for you to stretch out your arms
to include all people.

Believing

It was not just Thomas
who found it difficult
to believe in you, Jesus.

After you walked out of the tomb,
you talked with Mary Magdalene—
and she hurried to tell
your sorrowing followers.

But they would not believe her.

Nor would they believe the two
who hurried back to Jerusalem
to report that you had walked with them
and broken bread with them.

You had to go yourself
to where these followers were gathered
so that they would know
that you are truly the Holy One of God.

To where we are gathered,
come now, Jesus.

Dress for Success

When you were born,
your mother and father wrapped you
in a long strip of cloth.

You grew up
wearing the simple clothes
of a carpenter's son.

Throughout your ministry
you walked the dusty roads
of Judea and Samaria and Galilee,
clothed as a person of the land.

After the soldiers
put you on the cross,
they cast lots
for your humble clothing.

And when you died,
your friends took you
down from the cross
and wrapped you
in a long strip of cloth.

The Donkey

Mary,
heavy with child,
climbed up onto the donkey
for the long, slow ride
to Bethlehem.

And again
she climbed up,
holding her baby close to her,
with Joseph walking at her side,
for the journey
down into the safety of Egypt.

And she climbed up yet again
for their return,
after the death of Herod,
to the little village of Nazareth.

Again she rode the donkey
on the journeys,
spring after spring,
to the Feast of the Passover
in Jerusalem.

Until at last you, Jesus,
heavy with knowing,
climbed up onto the donkey
for the long, slow journey
down the palm-strewn street
that led in time
to the upper room

and Gethsemane,
to the house of the high priest
and Pilate's headquarters
and Calvary.

The Troubled Family of Jesus

The scandal sheets
at the grocery check-out counter
could run some interesting stories
about the people
in your family tree, Jesus.

I can see the headlines
about some of your ancestors
listed in the first chapter of Matthew:

"Abraham was the father of Isaac"
SON PONDERS FATHER'S ATTEMPT TO SACRIFICE HIM

"Isaac the father of Jacob"
SON TRICKS FATHER OUT OF BROTHER'S INHERITANCE

"Jacob the father of Judah and his brothers"
SONS SELL BROTHER INTO SLAVERY

And what about the women?

"Judah the father of Perez and Zerah, whose mother was Tamar"
WOMAN TRICKS FATHER-IN-LAW INTO IMPREGNATING HER

"Salmon the father of Boaz, whose mother was Rahab"
PROSTITUTE AIDS TWO SPIES

"Boaz the father of Obed, whose mother was Ruth"
MAN WEDS FORBIDDEN FOREIGN WOMAN

"David was the father of Solomon, whose mother
had been Uriah's wife"
KING SENDS SOLDIER TO FRONT LINE
AND CERTAIN DEATH, STEALS WIFE

Jesus, your family
was almost as troubled
as ours.

Well-being

Your Word: a laser
touching our inner beings,
healing our spirits.

Psalm 119:11

Your information
I've stored in my database,
keeping me on line.

Places of Honor

As Salome,
the mother of James and John,
stood at the foot of the cross
and saw the two men
on the crosses beside you, Jesus,
did she remember
that she had asked if her two sons
could be with you—
one on your right
and one on your left?

And did she know that
in the days to come,
her two sons,
as they witnessed for you,
would indeed be alongside you
in suffering?

The Call

Jesus,
if you had come to us
and called us
to be among your disciples,
we could have spent each day
listening to you,
talking with you,
going with you,
and helping you
as you did your work.

We believe that you call us
to do these same things today.

Thank God for Friday

Jesus, you showed us
the full extent of your love
for us one Friday.

When We Look at the Cross

What do we feel, Jesus,
when we look at the cross?

Horror,
guilt,
sorrow.

The only way
we can look at the cross
is to remember
not what we feel,
but what you felt
for us:
love.

The Promise

Jesus, you have promised
to be with your people always,
even to the end of the world.

So we understand
the Who (you),
the When (with us always),
the Where (even to the
farthest place on earth).

But what about the What
and the Why and the How?

What do you do when you're with us?
And Why? And How?

You told your followers
to make disciples of all people,
baptizing them
and teaching them
all that you've taught us.

So the What is that you're with us,
not just for companionship,
but to give us the power
to do your work with you.

The Why is that you love not only us
but all people,
and call us to reach out to them.

And the How is that through us,
unworthy though we are,
you do your work in this world.

Give Us

Jesus, after the Last Supper,
when you said your farewell
to your disciples
and summed up all
you'd been trying to tell them,
you spoke much
about joy.

You knew what
you were facing
and yet you told them
you wanted them
to have your joy.

You wanted them to have it
in full measure
and to ask in your name
so that their joy
might be complete.

Give us also
this joy.

Perhaps

Jesus, what do you think
about those of us
who call ourselves your people
and then go to war with each other?

What do you think
about our
 shooting,
 mining,
 and bombing each other?

About our
 gassing,
 and strafing each other?

About our
 bayoneting each other?

Perhaps those of us
who call ourselves your people
could stop killing each other.

Hostility

Jesus, you were born in a barn
because no one was willing
to make room for you.

While you were still an infant,
you and your parents fled as refugees
to escape the soldiers
Herod sent to kill you.

In the little town where you grew up,
the people wanted to
throw you off a cliff.

Throughout your ministry
the rulers of the temple,
jealous of the way the people
were flocking to hear you,
looked for ways to do away with you.

Finally they did kill you
at the village dump,
out beyond the edge of human habitation.

I'm Afraid We've Thought . . .

First we'll take care
of important things,
then we might stop to wonder
for a few moments
what life is all about.

First we'll make sure
we have everything we want,
then we might notice if
others are in need.

As long as things
are all right for us,
we won't get too upset
if others are not treated justly.

The View from the Cross

What did the world
  look like, Jesus,
as you gazed down
  from the cross?

Did you see how we
  scramble for possessions,
  caring more about things
  than about people,
as you watched the soldiers
  cast lots for your clothing?

Did you see how we
  have little concern for others
  and heap scorn upon those
  less fortunate than ourselves,
as passersby taunted you?

Did you see how we
  don't care enough to
  challenge established ways
  of doing things,
  even though those ways
  may be cruel,
as the crowd let you
  be impaled
  on two rough pieces of wood?

A Person of Little Significance

You were certainly
one of the most unimportant people
anyone could imagine.

You were born
an illegitimate child.

You spent your infancy
as a homeless person.

You later lived in a
run-down little village
about which people asked,
"Can anything good
come out of that town?"

You were raised in a family
that had little
of this world's wealth.

As an adult,
you roamed the countryside,
never seeming to settle down.

The leaders of your day
considered you a person
that the world
would probably be better off without.

And they finally did away with you
by nailing you up
on some rough lumber.

You were certainly one of
the most insignificant people
anyone could imagine.

My Biggest Fear

Not of the bad that
might happen, but of the good
I'm afraid to do.

Letting Go

Jesus,
I'm kneeling
before some rough pieces of lumber
rammed into the ground
on a hill called Calvary.
I'm asking you
to take all the things
I've done that've hurt others
and that they've done that've hurt me
and that I've done that've hurt myself
and you.

I'm going to leave them all
here.

Thank you.

Passersby

Jesus, you grieve for
those oppressed, but far more for
those who walk on by.

The Two Jacobs

Both were fathers of a Joseph—
one in the Old Testament,
the other in the New.

Both were forebears of Jesus—
one the grandfather,
the other the great-grandfather
back thirty-eight generations.

One, well-known,
conniving—but committed—
the other, silent
throughout the pages of history.

One, awarding his son
a coat of various colors,
the other, raising his son
to be a carpenter
and a father to Jesus.

Both helping Jesus to be
a person of the people.

We're Wondering

As long as one child
is hungry, Jesus,
how can we eat in peace?

As long as one child shivers
for lack of warm clothing,
how can we go through
our days in comfort?

As long as one child
has no place to lay its head,
how can we sleep in peace?

For you, Jesus,
are always
that one child.

Fishing

Jesus went to Galilee
to begin his ministry
with a folk whose hope had fled
    and faith grown dim.

And he issued there his call,
"Simon, Andrew, leave it all."
And at once they dropped their nets
    and followed him.

Then he walked along the shore
and he stopped to gather more
fisherfolk to help him bring
    the great catch in.

"James and John, come follow me
and we'll fish a different sea."
And at once they dropped their nets
    and followed him.

Jesus walks the shore today
calling us to walk his way.
We can hardly hear his voice
    above the din.

And he calls, "Come, follow me,
and you fisherfolk will be."
And at once we drop our nets
    and follow him.

What Would We Do?

What would we do, Jesus,
if you had never come?

We would have lost our way.

We would have lacked for truth.

We'd never have found life.

For you are our way
and our truth
and our life.

What would we do, Jesus,
if you had never come?

From God

Jesus,
we believe
you've come from God.

How else could you
have said the things
you said?

Or have done the things
you did?

Or have been
who you were
and are?

Jesus,
we believe
you've come from God.

Gifts

Jesus, whatever we
  have given to you
you have given back
  in greater measure,
  brimming full,
  spilling over.

What have we done
  with what you
  have given to us?

On That Day

You will not have to
say a word, Jesus,
when we stand before you
on that day.

When we see how you care
for each of us,
you will not have to
remind us of the times
that we hurt others.

All our selfishness
will fall away
as you look at us.

Your Call

You call us, Jesus,
to follow you every hour,
not in spare moments.

Centering

Purity of heart
is to will one thing: to seek
to center in you.

Necessities

We take for granted, Jesus,
that we should have
all the fanciest food
that we want,
plenty of clothes—
more than we need—
a fine place to live,
and lots of interesting things to do.

By the time
we take care of all these,
it's sometimes difficult
to find the time
to do your work with you.

You Have Shown Us

Jesus, you have shown us
how to live with others.

You have opened for us
a whole new way
of looking at other people
and being with them.

You have shown us
life.

Pass It Along

So many people
have helped us, Jesus. Help us
be there for others.

What Are You Doing Today?

We know that when you
were here on earth, Jesus,
you spoke about God's loving community
that's coming
and that's already here among us.

We know that you were concerned
about those who were hungry,
sick, or oppressed,
and that you helped them.

Are you trying to do
the same things today
through those of us you've called
to follow you?

Because

Because you love me, Jesus,
I know that you don't
want other people to hurt me.

And because you love other people,
I know that you don't want me
to hurt them.

This is not too difficult
to understand.

It's just difficult
to live up to.

Only in you
do we find the strength
to try.

Translation

The book of Ephesians begins:
"Paul, messenger of Jesus Christ
by the will of God. . . ."

Jesus, we're wondering:
In place of Paul's name,
would it be all right
if we inserted ours?

What Are We Doing?

Are we spending our days
in a world that's hungry
    making sure we're fed sumptuously?

In a world that's huddled in the cold
    making sure we're elegantly housed and clothed?

In a world that's crying out in pain
    making sure we're endlessly entertained?

What are we doing?

When

We don't know, Jesus,
when the hour will be,
or where,
or how.

But we know
that you will be there
waiting for us.

At Harvest

We gather at harvest
the feast of abundance
to bring to our Father
our thanks and our praise
for bright golden wheatfields
and green-purple vineyards
that bring the communion
of your love and grace.

We thank you the most,
Jesus Christ, for your friendship.
You came to invite us,
from greatest to least,
to come and sit down
and rejoice, all together,
as sisters and brothers
at Heaven's great feast.

New Hope

Jesus, because you came
we see our world
in a new way:

Not part bad,
part good,
and headed for destruction,

But blessed by your presence
and waiting for
your new creation.

We're Chosen

This our joy, our life:
not that we chose you, but that
you have chosen us.

It's Coming

We're working up
an appetite
for Heaven's great feast,
when folk will come
from north and south
and from west and east,
from mountain high
and valley low—
our day's work all done—
and all sit down
together there
as one people—one.